The World, the Flesh, and Angels

Barnard New Women Poets Series
Edited by Christopher Baswell and Celeste Schenck

THE WORLD, THE FLESH, AND ANGELS

Mary B. Campbell

With an Introduction by Carolyn Forché

Beacon Press   Boston

Beacon Press
25 Beacon Street
Boston, Massachusetts 02108

Beacon Press books
are published under the auspices of
the Unitarian Universalist Association of Congregations.

96 95 94 93 92 91 90 89   8 7 6 5 4 3 2 1

Portions of this work have appeared in the following publications:
Agni Review: "Justice"; *The Atlantic:* "Money"; *Ex Libris:* "Folksong,"
"Precipitation," "Whatever I Want"; *The Little Magazine:* "Noise,"
"A Case of Mistaken Identity," "Aubade Solo," "Sympathy"; *Nantucket
Review:* "Elegy"; *Paris Review:* "Drugs," "The Loneliness of Men
Bathing"; *Partisan Review:* "Fear of Travel."

Text design by Lisa Diercks

Library of Congress Cataloging-in-Publication Data
Campbell, Mary B.
    The world, the flesh, and angels.
    (Barnard new women poets series)
    I. Title.   II. Series.
PS3553.A486W67   1989   811'.54   88-47882
ISBN 0-8070-6806-3
ISBN 0-8070-6807-1 (pbk.)

In memory of my mother,
Jeanne Farrell Campbell

Contents

III

Acknowledgments

I am grateful to many people—friends, teachers, students, my editors, Chris Baswell and Celeste Schenck of the Barnard New Women Poets Series, Joanne Wyckoff and Thomas Fischer at Beacon Press. But it's the poets who have made me and kept me a poet: Stephanie Bobo, Gerald Fitzgerald, Robert Hahn, Joshua Kaplan, Sheila King, George Starbuck, and Melinda Weinstein have read my poems and shown me theirs; S. E. Carlisle, Carolyn Forché, Helaine Ross, Jenny Wilson, and most of all Larry Breiner helped me put this book together.

Introduction
Carolyn Forché

As children we were given the gift of angelic protection, a guardian spirit assigned to each of us, and in our imagination it was therefore possible to conceive a host of such presences standing or kneeling beside our school desks, hovering above us, transparent and therefore invisible in their vigilance. During the years of our adulthood, acknowledgment of such presences disappeared. The angels who had accompanied us, keeping us under benevolent spiritual surveillance, were meant in our maturity to dwell within us as reason and conscience, still radiant and protective but no longer magnificently winged. Theological contemplation of angels drifted to the periphery of spiritual attention. If lately there has been a resurgence of interest in the hosts of heaven, with their choirs of seraphim and cherubim, thrones, powers, dominions, virtues, principalities, archangels, and angels, it might be because we have remembered that they were not only our guardians but also messengers of God. Our renewed interest in celestial immortals may mean that we have sensed an abyss before us and wish to reach the safety of a postnuclear world without having to pass through the annihilation of the human world, its memory and future, as well as its imagination of a safe foothold beyond nuclear self-destruction. With *The World, the Flesh, and Angels,* Mary Campbell has begun a brilliant poetic articulation of this collective fear and the intuitively responsive desire for collective redemption.

In his most recent film, *Wings of Desire,* Wim Wenders offers us a contemporary Berlin of bleak worker housing blocks and cleared ruins where angels dwell among humans, recording their subvocal symphony of concerns. The presence of such "recording angels" might suggest a way in which to think about Mary Campbell's work. She recognizes the world as before an abyss that is personal, social, political, and whose fate determines the fate of the flesh, seen as at once vulnerable and burdensome. In her vision, angels are with us and may at times inhabit us as the "perfect stranger" reason has become. An angelic murmur rises through this book, a soft dissonant aria of human pathos and angelic intercession. Here is a poet who perceives the increasing velocity of human life, its building momentum, a poet who is conscious of the erasure of memory, the totalizing impulse and the abandonment of the body, an impulse to step from the flesh as if from articles of clothing, to remove the flesh and become spirit, a desire for annihilation from which who but angels could save us.

In a reversal of the Adamic rite of naming the creatures of the earth, Mary Campbell calls them forth through the prefiguring veil of a forest fire which takes the lives of egrets, pelicans, armadillos, lilies, palmettos, alligators, oranges, moss, and scorpions. Later Campbell writes of an earth "so hot / The lizards have to dance to stay alive." Her "recording angel" monitors not the naming of creatures but their extinction. When she turns to the Scriptures, it is to Lot's wife, turning not only for a final glimpse of the conflagration, a simple act of witness, but because upon hearing the first screams as they "swept across the empty plain / Like a question," she wants to answer them.

From this poetry, obsessed with light, with life after life and after death, with love, which is "the breaking of all spells," and heaven ("an equation / Containing thirty variables"), we learn that "Grief comes from the word / For North, and the word for weight," that this is an earth that "loses everything," as does the flesh which becomes gossamer, having been "eaten away by love." Few contemporary poets have offered so discerning a vision of our condition or understood so well the acceleration of human life and the effect of speed on landscape and consciousness. "We keep waking to higher speed limits," she writes.

> Only an operator at the speed of light
> Could clear this manic screen
> But we try. Time is the mercy of the Fall:
> If we go fast enough
> We may just rise again.

We are, for this moment, in a video game where

> Atari and Intelevision are adjusting us
> To immortality. . . .
> . . . .
> At each stage of the video game
> We move faster, score fewer hits.
> It's harder to win as it goes along,
> Harder just to survive. The enemy
> Divides and subdivides, and even multiplies

While we fly anxiously among the bombs and stars,
Sole focus of a universe designed
For our annihilation.

Poised before so abstract a precipice, Campbell does not abandon the world or sacrifice her humor. She shows us movies (*Ran; Aguirre, the Wrath of God*), a cartoon ("The Jetsons"), and permits us within the imagination of Richard Nixon. She addresses economic inequity inventively in a poem called "Money," in which she admonishes us that "life / Is too short to waste / On being poor" and therefore "We need to give each other money / Till we are rich beyond our wildest dreams." *The World, the Flesh, and Angels* resolves itself with warnings, instructions, and a suggestion that people who write on walls are trying to tell us something. There are no accidents in this purely accidental world. The stars can be read "like tea leaves."

"Stop grieving," she tells us, "Try on rage." Or we will perhaps share sleep's "final dream / A song without words, and no one singing it."

I

The Perfect Gaze: An Admonition

Great care must be taken in looking
At the beloved. If you look
Too long, the spirit of the other
Will be forced into hiding
Or disappear from this world.
The gaze must be no longer
Than five glances; otherwise
It is fatal.

The gaze should be empty of design
Or content: it is like a question
Which is satisfied at every moment.
Even in sleep, the face of the other
Forestalls the need to know more.
If you ask out loud
You will waken a liar.

Ending the gaze is a rupture:
You look away, you abandon the beloved
You travel inwardly. This is freedom
And the hardest part. But love
Is the breaking of all spells,
Even its own.

Scientific Explanations

You can spot the blind a mile away
With their sunken eyes and faces pale as day
And that look of utter innocence
And the nimbus where light flutters
Protective and abashed—I guess you could say
That light tries harder with the blind

Their secret has been kept a long time
But I know it: they are the angels
That's why they look so kind
God must have forgotten, when he sent them here
To this dull, sublunary sphere
That in our virtual darkness they'd be as good as blind

But they don't complain
They work in broom factories and they chant his name
And when they stand and wait for the subway train
They smile as if the clouds were parting
And a chariot coming down
To take them out of town

The cherubim and the seraphim have dogs
The rest of the hierarchy gets by with canes
You don't believe me—
You thought they'd be huge, and have wings
And hover about fifteen feet above us in a kind of golden fog
Speak Hebrew and know impossible things

You can go right on thinking that if you like
If it doesn't seem obvious to you, maybe I'm wrong
Maybe the world is intolerably bright
And the blind, like baby kittens, can't take it yet
Or maybe they're in love with light
And playing hard to get

Fuseli's The Blind Milton

The Blind Milton is almost invisible,
Greenfaced in the shadows wearing black,
His death's head thrown back by a trance
Or a vision worse than his blindness.
At his right hand stands an odalisque
In white, his daughter, slouching
Over a podium, her bare neck bent
And gleaming in a shaft of strong light.

Is she taking dictation? Is she reading to him?
Is he listening to her? Is he imagining
The way she looks? Is she the light
Gone out of his eyes and made flesh?
I wonder what he would think
Of the revealing cut of her dress
Or the sly smile on her parted lips.
Does he know she has secretly learned Greek
And that she has begun to alter a phrase,
Here and there, in his poem?

A Case of Mistaken Identity

I soaked the seaweed in a crystal bowl
Unfolded it carefully, like an insect making lace
Cut it into strands on the chopping block
And then into tiny squares, for tomorrow's soup.
It was midnight. The angels' murmuring grew louder in my ear
So I picked through the rice, pulling out all the unhusked kernels
And the black ones, and the dead white ones
And the burnt red ones that hurt your teeth
And rinsed what remained, though I could hear them coming
In their shining spiritual armor
And put it in a loaf pan to soak overnight
Though I feared that by morning the rice and I
And my lover, who was watching me
In delight, would be reduced to ash.
The horns, the cymbals, the terrible percussion of the host
Rattled the windows, so I mashed the chick peas and mustard
Collateral against the pillar of flame
That lighted my work, but not
Thank heavens, the innermost secrets of my soul.
My lover saw nothing but a woman doing a woman's work for
    him.
When I lifted a stone and placed it on the pickles I had started
He could not see the burning foot of Raphael
Light on it, nor hear the explosion
Of the rock in my heart
Nor smell the flesh of my neck
Singed where the Thrones and Dominations
Grasped it: he thought I was bowing my head to him.

Elegy

When I get old
I will no longer be an egomaniac
The wild deer will feed out of my hand
And if I am adored
I will not care

I will have stopped reading by then
And my thin Celtic skin will be a mass
Of wrinkles, a calendar
For impatient devotees: I will not look
In the mirror either

The bottle of perfume
I presently keep in the bathroom
Will one day run out, even though
I thin it with water
Near the end

And then I will be able
Secretly to enter all rooms
Even the forest
Without frightening
Or pleasing anyone

Life after Life

At each stage of the video game
We move faster, score fewer hits.
It's harder to win as it goes along,
Harder just to survive. The enemy
Divides and subdivides, and even multiplies
While we fly anxiously among the bombs and stars,
Sole focus of a universe designed
For our annihilation. Even destruction
Brings no rest: in the video game
We have nine lives and no karma.
Atari and Intelevision are adjusting us
To immortality, the latest thing.
Life in the fast lane is no joke:
No slouch can bear it, and it never ends.
We keep waking to higher speed limits,
Keener engines; the hand on the joystick,
Knee-jerk tightrope-walker and survivalist,
Blows everything it can out of the sky.
Only an operator at the speed of light
Could clear this manic screen
But we try. Time is the mercy of the Fall:
If we go fast enough
We may just rise again.

Theseus and Ariadne, or, The First Telephone

The silk thread trembled
All through the stone
Halls of the maze.
Did it mean a killing
At the center,
Or the impatient
Shudder of the girl
At the door?
There is no clue
But this silk
Sentence of life.
Read forwards or backwards
It says, "We are both
Holding on."

A Long Pause in a Contemporary Song

What'll we do? What'll we do?
There isn't any sound at all!
The conductor looks like a statue
You can hear the dust motes fall.

I'm on the edge of my seat
Counting: eleven measures now
Or is it minutes? I'm listening
To nothing and I don't know how.

No one has spoken, or fainted
Or fallen asleep again
Or taken a deep breath, or stirred.
Nobody knows when

If ever, the singer will resume.
We know just one thing, but we can prove it:
This isn't the end. Our silence means
That other silence must be music.

The Goldberg Variations

The harpsichord is annoyingly inexpressive
And the music a series of sentences
About cell division or heat death
In another language.
We have gotten too dumb and passionate
To follow this.

I close my eyes. The vernal equinox
Is upon us, but I forget that.
The heart disappears, and then the nerves.
There is nothing left of me. I sleep.

The fourteenth variation, a beebop exercise
Strikes me as insane: an old German typewriter
Tries to adapt to the jungle, clatters
And swings in moist darkness
Then rusts to a halt.

I dream: the notes proliferate
A meticulous waterfall
A liquid city, engineered to last.

I am climbing its transparent girders
Bridges, stairwells; I am lost
Among towers intricate as lace
In a maze of air, in the brain
Of an angel.

I have no mother, no lover, no home.
I come trailing clouds of glory
From heaven, which is an equation
Containing thirty variables, enclosed
In arias as dull and true as sleep.

Lines Written a Few Inches from The Cathedral at Rouen

This is not a cathedral.
It is a bunch of little dabs
Of colored mud. Many of the dabs
Are mud-colored.
This is not three o'clock
In the afternoon at the end
Of the nineteenth century
Any more than the phone
That rings in the movie
Is for you. If this is like
Anything, it is not
A midafternoon cathedral
But you yourself:
A kaleidoscope of mud
Whose seething arabesques
Seem, at a distance,
Massive, shapely, whole.
Across the room, bored children
On a field trip recognize
A cathedral and see,
Without caring, exactly
How unhappy you must be.

Double Exposure: To a Man in a Chair, Reflected

With your back to the mirror
You can say anything
In any voice, you can lie
You can make things up
You can change your name
You can even refuse to answer.

With your back turned
He cannot see you. He can,
It is true, imagine you
As an image of his own
Curve in the chair, the outline
Of his sensation, but he cannot
Read your lips, nor can
You know what he is thinking.

Stripping: A Romance

Let's undress, and let's take it
To excess, I mean take off
Everything we have on,
Everything we ever had on,
Even the bodies we think we have,
Even the bodies our mothers had.

First we take off our apartments
Room by room, tossing them
Into the corner like garters
Because we are so strong,
So strong we could take off
Whole temples if we had to.

We stand panting, in the open air
Facing each other in our coats.
The wind is cruel, and so is the rain
But we have such courage now:
We tear off our coats as if
We were drowning in the river.

My dress, your sweater, your jeans
Just flotsam now; the flesh
is hardest to remove. We hold
Our heads above the water
For the longest time. The talk dies down
At last, and we go under.

Angels are really naked—
We don't even have souls
To cover us. We interpenetrate
All day, all night. We have taken off
The river, and the memory of it.
We are perfect strangers.

Life after Death

I was amazed to discover the angels
Telling dead baby jokes over their cornflakes.
"Ubi sunt . . ." I sighed, and wept.
They barely noticed.

Life after death has been a challenge
Of a peculiar kind:
I am not even sure, for instance,
That I *am* dead . . . I still get hay fever
And sneeze explosively at times.

I had imagined something different—
A kind of geometric purity
And thinness to this sphere, or at least
An odor of the occult, altar roses
A feverish and splendid inactivity.

It is still a shock to me, when I go walking
The green street of Paradise
To see Saint Theresa in her office window
At work, as ever, on the account books
Of a long defunct monastic institution
Whose passing was not noted here
Where the leaves fall like lead weights
In the wrong season, and the sun forgets,
Quite frequently, to sink.

Down Under

Desire is a careless skater
Near the center of the lake.
Pure joy has set her spinning,
Face raised, eyes pinned
To the spinning center
Of the sky-blue sky.

Alone, this close to heaven,
Who but a coward
Would have noticed that the ice
Is darker at the spindle
Of the world? Who could remember
What that means?

Desire has fallen through.
In the dark water, freezing,
Her slow hands stroke,
By accident, the sleeping fish.

The Loneliness of Men Bathing

No one bothers to imagine men in baths.
None of us sitting home alone
On a dull, rainy evening
Thinks of the nude male body
Half-floating, eyes closed, in scented water
Littered with petals, loosening himself
Into the liquid grace of muscular abandon,
One arm perhaps draped over the bath's edge
Beckoning unconsciously, the left hand
Drawing a long, slow line along
The silkened, opened, underwater skin
Of an upper thigh until it reaches
Tactile complications at the loins
And just gets lost.

The lovely self-involvement of this wet
Body, slightly stirring, aromatic,
Weightless, gorgeous, given up to pleasure
Is no secret, but still the event
Goes unattended, night after night
Year after year.
People imagine something else; men rise
From dirty, unimagined water
Put on an old bathrobe
Make tea and clip their nails
Without so much applause
As a single caught breath
Or pair of widened eyes.

O fragrant, oiled Odysseus, O Marat
Interrupted, O Bloom in your indolent tub,
O Christ in heaven and your feet
In Mary Magdalene's hair, forgive me!
Think of me, from now on, thinking of you—
Vigilant, breathless, crazy with desire.

Voyeur

I am staring across the river
At the Riverside Press building
Curving like a comma
In its million bricks, shining
Like a scimitar
In its thousand windows, bending
North right where the shining
River bends south
Like the long-haired girl
Bends jitterbugging from her bending
Man. The warehouse is empty.
The river is starting to freeze.
The student at my office door
Is murmuring politely
But I cannot hear her:
I am thinking with all my heart
How it is to love this way—
Empty and shining and bending away—
And how beautiful the molten
Metal of the freezing river
Looks, even now, without
Its swans, shining
And bending away.
My student has no idea
How much I can love, no idea
I am doing it in front of her.

"I LOVE YOU"

About a year after she helped me move
My friend found eight love letters
Under the back seat of her car
Addressed to me. They appeared
To have been soaked in cooking oil
And the edges shattered in my hands
Like mica. Fragments that said "you"
And "to you" and "with you"
Gathered on the counter as I tried
To unfold them. The letters were ten years old.
I didn't actually read them, but I couldn't
Help noticing on one of them block letters
Three inches high that said "I LOVE YOU."
Earlier that day I had been thinking
How love was a great net of golden threads
That caught a fish or a crab
Or an old bottle or a drift of weed
Or whatever there was. A letter,
Eight letters. There is nothing of value
In the sea but these great gold nets
Shimmering and sinking.

Searchlights

Love never ends
But I have seen it moving—
Seen many loves, crisscrossed
In the night sky,
Sweeping the dark.

What a show! What distances
Of air, what giant gazes
Meet and lock, above so many acres
Of the dim city,
Of pasture, of water.

When the beams are long
The crossing is long too:
Marriage. Celestial X's
Cancel the stars, straightening
Slowly into pairs of I's.

When a beam points straight up
It has no focus
But the universe. Its light
Blends into the dark, a pious
Widow, dying very old.

Chronicle

The monks among the reeds
And the geese on the shore
Of the lake or river
Where deer drink, where cattle come
To find the sweetest grass:
These gather to make history.
Brown geese, brown habits
Blur in early mist, on fallow earth
Under a dun cloud. Violence and art
Will uproot, pluck and skin these vegetables
And animals; gall in the water
Will be ink. On flesh side and hair side
Goose quills and reeds inscribe the words of the dead
On the skins of the dead
So nothing will be lost.

The Afterlife

Not heaven, not coming back
Seethrough and scary
Or someone else, and not
The hard jewelry of bones
At fathom five.

What I want is still life:
Peaches in a blue bowl
An opened lemon on the linen
Tablecloth, a little knife
White-edged with sunlight
From a window open
To the summer just beyond
The frame.

The room is not empty.
Someone has eaten
The ripest peach and left.
Her happiness illuminates
Each molecule of fruit
And steel and linen, every grain
Of pigment, every wave
Of citron, cerulean, vermilion
Gray and chinese white.

Dust hangs over the table
In the light, still
And perpetual as angels
Who will not return to dust.

II

An Etymology

Grief comes from the word
For North, and the word for weight.
It is a later word. Long ago
It was more important to say where,
Or how much, than to say
The thing we say when we say grief
Now that we say it.

I'm full of grief, but the wind
Is from the West and I weigh
Almost nothing. Nothing oppresses me
In this free country, in August,
And the open grave is empty.
I have no excuse.

One day in the past, someone
Discovered gravity. He was hauling
A great weight to the graveyard,
Breasting a north wind, and his heart
Broke suddenly, and totally.
If anyone had asked, he would have said
The words for "North" and for "heavy."
No one would understand. He would die there,
Glued to the earth, and cold, and crazy
To find the word for what else
It was that killed him.

Impressionism

> And in the Roche whithinne the chapell yet ap-
> paren the fyngres of oure lordes hond whan he
> putte hem in the roche when the Jewes wolden
> have taken him. And fro then a stones cast toward
> the south is another chapell where oure lorde
> swette drops of blood.
> —*Mandeville's Travels*

Jesus must have weighed a ton.
In a field outside Cairo he made seven wells
With one of his feet, while he was still a child
Playing with the other children.
He left his mark on everything.
Barefoot, he littered the hard rocks of Palestine
With footprints that are still there today
And his fingerprints were like bulletholes.
Even the hoofprints of his ass remain, at the Golden Gate
Where he entered Jerusalem on Palm Sunday.
His blood changed the color of the Temple's stone floor
And his face was so bright it left a photograph
On Veronica's kerchief, 1900 years before Eastman.

No matter where we turn the land is changed,
Inscribed, memorial. The proofs are everywhere
And everywhere he walked, or leapt
Or simply stood
Is dyed or dented or emblazoned.
A heavier man, with brighter blood
Or more electric eyes, there never was.
This was the artist who need never wonder,
Should he sign his work?
The pressures of his body signed the world.

Breaking the Fast

for Larry Breiner

The first light of dawn is cold
And hard to tell apart from night
But for the one star
That grows dim instead of bright
And, in the distance, the roar
Of hungry lions.

The zoo is only a mile away
And the lions are ravenous
As clockwork.

I get up in the near dark
And go out, to stand
With my feet in the dew and feel,
Startled as ever by the trauma
With which the day begins.

What is it like to be so hungry,
To be driven to a roar
While the dew still hangs in your mane?
You can see the breath from their red mouths
On the hillside, rising, tangled
Among the tame little trees.

You can hear their hearts pounding with desire
While the sun bleeds over the horizon,
A far and odorless carcass
Its cool spirit filling the sky
Lighting the world
Lighting the keepers' faces as they trudge forward,
Trembling, with their burden of meat.

Buttons

The miniature horse at the Topsfield Fair
Weighed forty-eight pounds. "A miracle"
Said the signs, and it only cost
$1.05 to get in and see it.
Buttons stood like a lady in his box,
Posed and miserable, his hooves turned out,
His eyes as vapid and liquid
As the swamp in which he seemed to drown
Steadily. He insisted on dying.
When he went to his pail of water
It was only to reconfirm
How small he was. He was so small
A chicken could have broken his back.
He was too small to have sex
And too beautiful to live without it.

Your Fish Phobia

for Jenny Wilson

Why are you afraid of what lives
In the water? Is it the thought of life
That doesn't seem to breathe?
Do you imagine the strange shapes
The octopus takes, or the eel,
Are ways to express a life-long
Suffocation? That the fin
And the tentacle search for air?
Do you fear the speechlessness of fish?

When we saw the dead ray
On the beach, did you scream
In pity? Because it had reached
Our heaven, and had choked here?
Because it had tried to utter
Words of praise, and found too late
It didn't have a mouth?

From the Amtrak Roomette, Christmas Eve, as My Train Passes through a Forest Fire at 70 Mph

> And say to the south forest: Hear the word of the Lord: thus saith the Lord God: Behold I will kindle a fire in thee, and will burn in thee every green tree, and every dry tree: the flame of the fire shall not be quenched: and every face shall be burned in it, from the south even to the north.
> —*Ezekiel 20:47*

Midnight, the heart of Florida,
Dry trees and green alike aflame
In full moonlight; fire
Like a plague of poppies, blossoms
Tossing in a slight breeze;
Animals rampant and unhoused
And unrepentant, wings and tails
Outstretched: the train I'm on
Moves faster than all these.

Blessed be God that I was born
In time, and late enough,
To see this from the safety of my train—
Kneeling on my dry bones
With seventy miles per hour
Between me and the burning faces
Of the pelicans and egrets
And the armadillos
And the lilies of the field,
Burning, burning.

The new dawn comes up kindled
Over the safe and celebrating world of men.
We made it! Far behind the train
A host of bones, singed every color,
Hisses and sizzles for us in the dew.
Scape-egrets, scape-pelicans,
Scape-armadillos, scape-lilies,
Palmettos, alligators, oranges,

Scape-Spanish moss and scorpions
Gave up our ghost.
Come, spirit, from the four winds,
Blow upon these slain
And let them live again.

Justice

Lot's wife hurried on with a few things in a bag
In the rubble of the desert. The dirt and the rocks
Were as red as the sky. She had never run
So fast, or carried so much, and still
It wasn't fast enough, and she had had to leave
Most of her stuff at home. Ashes
Got in her eyes and pebbles in her shoes,
And she couldn't keep up with Lot
Or the two girls, who had already
Forgotten their fiancés.
It was almost dawn, a time
She had always had to herself—
Out in the yard, by the ovens,
Humming, she made bread
And listened for the earth to rise
On its many wings, with its conflicting songs.
The patter of brimstone in the distance
Quickened, and the first screams
Swept across the empty plain
Like a question which, in tears,
She turned to answer.

An Allegory of Love

In my father's Valentine card
Charlie Brown is trying to make one.
He is cutting a piece of red paper
Into the shape of a heart.
The work is not going well.
His hand shakes, and the outline
Is so ragged it seems to have teeth.
He cuts and cuts, trying to smooth it,
Make it respectable: he should
Have used a stencil. It keeps
Getting smaller as he spirals inward
Toward the ideal shape,
But it always looks the same; it looks
As if he'd made it with a chain saw.
Red scraps collect in front of him
Like biopsies. At last there is nothing left.

Love is the shaking hand, the scissors,
The shape that eludes them both.
The scraps that conclude the process
Might be reassembled by a genius
But my father lets them be. He signs, as always
With a question mark.

Nostalgia

Mrs. Jetson wears a Burger King pantsuit.
She is so fecund she can make dinner
Come out of the wall. Her husband
Comes home in a tiny airplane
And she clips and kisses him. She brings him
A space drink.

They have no time to talk, for here come
The children, those two and a half little terrors
And the dog Astro, a mutt,
A far cry from his grandfather the wolf
Who could have eaten this family for lunch
And been howling with hunger again by sundown.

George Jetson is literally bowled over
By his children and animals. They want
Him to do their math homework
They want a milkbone, they want the car.
He gives them everything; they go away
And he grabs Jane by the hairdo and takes her
Right there on the patio.

Afterwards as they lie staring over the parapet
Into a deep twilight, empty at last of aircraft,
They cry together, remembering their first date
In the multi-purpose room at the Middle School,
How green their faces seemed in the flourescent light,
How quickly they replaced each kiss.

A Panic

I'm sweating, it's terrible
I'm scared, you don't know
Erce erce erce, mother earth
Help me, turn me into snow

Swallows go hectic over my head
The radiator screams
I got no rhythm, the charm won't work
This is a bad dream

Only an oriental adept
Could have designed this tightrope
That comes to an end in mid-air:
I have to do my trick without hope

Nobody else does. Why is it
That the moon goes up and down twelve times
A night in my sky, and the stars pop
Like milkweed, filling my street with crimes?

If I could stop sweating long enough
I'd design a still red flower
Around which the universe turns
A hundred times an hour

And I'd go there and hide in it
At the still point
That's my idea of heaven
I wanna blow this joint

Starry Night

The furious peace of the stars
Fell over the mountain all at once
Illuminating nothing.

Beneath that brilliant net
Bears roamed deciduous darkness
Rummaging for garbage, live or dead.

Beneath that chaste jewelry
No moon rose naked, or showed
An arched white eyebrow over a dark eye.

Each star an angel, each constellation
A tyranny: the stars said what to do
Without a word, and we did.

The bears ate noiselessly
The men and women hid.

Eclogue

Love is easiest imagined
As a small animal surviving
In the territory of the wolf.
An animal who knows how to hide
And can forage under cover
Of daylight, and go for days
Without food.

In the pastoral there are no
Predators, and even so
The rabbits cower under the myrtle
And the finches sing
Their general alarm.

Love is easiest imagined
As a lone wolf on the crest
Of the hill in full moonlight
Whose yellow eyes miss nothing,
Who can do whatever he wants.

Sexual Terrorist

I want to be in a rock and roll band so bad.
I want to make my sins public
In a special little dress made of gold or fur
With one of those nuclear violins
Strapped on around my neck
And a couple thousand watts for a halo.
I want to make so much noise
That even God can't interrupt
And the 24-hour business of heaven
Just grinds to a halt, and the angels
Dangle in the sky like secretaries
In an air raid.
I want to make those tight wires
Scream under my hands like bombs
Dropping for miles over miles
Of empty Arizona sand, and whimper
Like animals when the sky goes black
And the scales stampede
And there's no cover to run for
Cause the cover's on fire and the earth is so hot
The lizards have to dance to stay alive.
And when I stop I'm gonna go backstage
Where it's real, real dark and take prisoners
All night. It could be you
Or anyone. Get ready.
If the ransom's rich enough I'll sing
That long, low note that makes the sun come up.

Confessed Witch

From my vile thicket in the north
Where amid a throng of brutal varmints
I read the stars like tea leaves
At the swamp's brim, I can tell
A few things, even in this strong darkness.

He is in another country.
He will find his fortune there
But he will not recognize it.
When he gets home, troubled in memory,
He will blame his sorrow on the climate.

Then he will come to me,
Imagining relief in this peculiar spot
Which daylight renders innocent.
Combing my hair under the yellowing birches,
I will seem too speechless and beautiful
To have brought him here by charms.

The ignorance of men
Is their real fortune.
From the very beginning
They have steered out of Paradise,
Hell-bent for True North
Where the sibyl huddles
With her bad intentions and her love.

Drugs

Coffee: the tightening at the heart,
The wreath of ice, like thorns
Arranged there to give pleasure,
The interpenetration of the nerves
And mind, until thought
Bites at your breast—keen lover
Or gourmand to a sentient peach.

A little later in life, not much,
Cold beer ungirdles that tight
Garland, turns the nerves to rivers,
Gives them sense of their own
Latent, riotous joyfulness, as if
They were in bed in fact, always in beds,
And by them willows loosing their long hair.

And oh, the cigarette: beyond
These sexual illusions, the pure bliss
Of smoke loved for its own sake,
The moment at which the body of man,
Alone among the animals,
Finds itself satisfied by nothing,
Or by a desire crafted to fulfill
A source of satisfaction.

Whatever I Want

> When you're making art you've got a page to fill,
> and you put in whatever you want.
> —*Nicholas, to his therapist*

On this page I want to see you
Lying in my lap, your face
Close enough for easy kisses,
Your eyes watching mine, and reading
What I have written here.

In the margins I want
The delicate grotesques of peace:
Cartoons of fat governments
Melting their swords
And drinking each other's native beer.

Between the lines, the beasts
Venture from their caves and lairs
To sniff our food. They know
We are too well fed to kill them.
They are intrigued by our strange ways.

Among the branching antlers
Of a gang of deer, my imaginary daughter
Learns to count. From the style
Of birdspeech she learns to keep time.
She will sing the budget to her lover.

At the top of the page, the title
Looms like a dawn. And tangled
In its rays, everything I think of
Is visible, and connected.
Whatever I want is true.

Aubade Solo

It's spring in December,
Jacket weather, false darkness
In a sky that is secretly bright:
Rain—something could happen
Just like this:

You are still asleep, not far
From the office. You think you're alone
Allowed to be ugly and elemental
But you're not. I'm right here
Not waiting but watching. I'll give you
Five more minutes to sleep.

Even that is hard—I have filled
In a flash your tree with cardinals
And set them singing.
I have blown a wind through it
And the branches hurl rain pebbles
At your window. Let the girl downstairs
Begin to practice on her guitar.
Let the trucks swish by with their
Sighing Doppler cadenza.
And now someone rings your bell
To get into the building:
Someone with antlers and wild eyes
With a torch, and a crucifix
Chanting a word of power.

Someone who has nothing on
Under her coat, who brought the rain
And birds to wake you utterly
Once and for all.
Someone that was like a cloud
Split open by the secret brightness
And is shining on you—
Your five minutes are up.

Folksong

Oh if only poems weren't fictions
If only encounters weren't dramas
If only we weren't all so inescapably
Good at civilization
If only ritual weren't as contagious
As syphilis.

You have no idea how much I want
To speak to you, dear reader
Dear flesh, dear blood, dear weeper
In the dark
You know very well I'm not speaking to you now
This is my act, and its only criterion
Is excellence.

Could we meet somewhere
By a river so wide, so wet, so lonely
With its one errant gull
And the moon in it like a torn love letter
And the willows starting to drown in it
Just meet there, at night, and say nothing
About it?

The Distance

The audience is more alive than you think
More alive than you are.
When you throttled Desdemona
It suffered immeasurably, while you tried to remember your next
    lines
And fought the temptation to interject an elephant joke.

Oh the pain in the audience went on forever
Charging through endless seas of grief
Like a healthy dolphin made immortal.
The curtain came down and you went backstage to strip
But the crowd has not forgotten your utter mistake
And is losing its religion, praying in continual frustration
That what you never did at all
Shall be undone.

Have pity on your audience, glued to their seats
Implicated in all your crimes:
Remember the man in Texas who shot and killed Othello from
    the back row.

Love and Death

I am asleep on the train
And I am safe because you
Are awake, thinking of me,
Keeping track of my distance,
Reeling me out into the dark.
I wake up between midnight
And dawn and your reel,
The moon, is huge and close
Over a snowy field. The train
Is shooting west at the same speed
As the eastbound fox
At whose heels an eastbound wolf
Pants with a fatal hunger.
The field is wide and long and the chase
Looks motionless, though it will end
In a violent death. It isn't true
That you love me. You are deep
In a dream of someone else
For whom you will run
Across the frozen waste so fast
Your heart will break.

Sympathy

The way my finch is acting
Since his wife died—starved
To death behind the *OED*—
Reminds me of my father:
I can feel the way he felt
In a slightly quieter house
Where there was suddenly
More light to go around, and yet
He still left her room in the bed,
Waited his turn in the shower,
By mistake, for hours.

When I get home at night
My finch and I join sadnesses,
Heads bent, mundane.
I hang my coat up, check the mail,
Say nothing, while Raoul
Flies twice about the room
Without parole. His grief arrives
In spurts, but steadily—
An SOS he mimics in his dull
Mechanical song. My heart,
A living carburetor, sings along.

Metonymy

I am moving to another city
And a widow is moving into my apartment.
On this day ten years ago
My father was widowed, and today
I got a postcard from a woman
About to be widowed in Scotland.
None of this explains why
I feel like a widow, too—why
I keep counting my friends to find
The missing one, why I am lonely
For someone I can't recall or imagine,
Stunned by an ache in a long-since
Excavated chamber of my heart.
All this widow data just gathers
Around me, like leaves in a doorway
At the start of that season
When the daughter is kidnapped
And the earth loses everything
In revenge.

Last Rites

Before he goes to bed, the count
Examines his ruby. He unwraps
It from its silk and feels it
And holds it up to the light. He sees
His room in it twenty times, blood red.
He watches the cat come toward him
Out of twenty other worlds.

The girl is in the bathroom
And the girl in the mirror
Is brushing her hair. The rhythm
Of the stare is undulant and slow.
Between locked eyes,
Only half real, dust scintillates
Unnoticed. Rapture comes.

The boy is saying goodnight to his newt
And there is an aunt with a rosary
Stepping into sleep on her knees.
Outside, the fox touches each
Of her cubs once. There is always
One more thing to do before the end.

A Refining Passion

I am simply being eaten away by love.
Already my body is gossamer,
Floats on my spirit with a barely legal transparence,
Clothes me like a dust mote clothes the light.

If you don't hurry it'll be too late.
I am going clear with hunger.
You can see right through my vacant heart,
My eyes are ragged holes
Torn in a cloud by wind.

Behind me the moon is still full
And bright, a point of order.
But the night will suck it down
As it has me—that ravenous henchman
Of invisibility.

Hurry. Hurry. I never wanted to be a breeze
Sighing impersonally in your ear,
A beige illumination
In an empty lot, the surface of a pool
Briefly disturbed with tears.

III

The Structure of Heavy Hydrogen

In critical piles across the farmlands
Of the West and Middle West the atoms wait
In blank indifference, happy just to be there
Spinning in place, harmonic. The night
Creeps over them like a strange cat
Blinking, roaming.

Each atom is a happy family; Mom and Dad are getting along fine
So far, and there is peace. They stay awake
All night, debating evenly. Mom believes
In God, and Dad does not. They are equally intelligent.

But the little neutrons know this is a hiatus.
Harmonies wait for resolution, and the tonic is war.
How long can this piece go on?
The cat gets bored, its eyes catch
The light of the harvest moon, its paws itch
To play ball. Every star is a multitudinous nation
Of families gone berserk, a blaze of divorces
From a distance beautiful, singing.

Money

We need more money.
There isn't enough, and life
Is too short to waste
On being poor.

Money in all its beautiful forms:
The pale wampum, the bright doubloon
Cowries blinking on the dawn shore
The tawny oxen, the rupee
With its ten colors.

We need to give each other money
Till we are rich beyond our wildest dreams
Until the banks of the world can't hold it
Until we have to melt it down into spoons.

There should be money on every tree
Nestled in the buds for safe keeping
Or in summer hanging heavy from the branches.
The leaves should clink as they fall
And the squirrels hoard nuggets of gold.

We could buy everything
If we had the money:
We could buy each other's freedom.
It would mean the end of rock and roll.
It would give us time to walk hand in hand
Through the forest with our lovers,
Like rich people do in a time of peace,
Naming the animals.

Heading for Trouble: A Scene from Ran

The man with no eyes is wearing
Sky-blue clothes and his sister
Is dressed like a toy, in pink
Satin and wind-colored gauze.
They move in the green field
Like very young children
Who have just learned to walk,
Of whom one has blindfolded
The other, and between whom
There is still an undivided trust.
The woman will soon be beheaded
In the ruined castle on the hill
Where they grew up. For now
They are awestruck at the nearness
Of their childhood home, and their stiff
Satin strikes exactly the right chord
With the stiff grasses
And the jerking, angular wind.
The sound is of paper, dry
And flexible. The colors
Are out of another world.
Hand in hand they lurch forward
In their fairytale clothes, and pause
And lurch forward again.
The woman can almost hear the grass
Rubbing the gray stone,
The blind man can almost see.

The deeper into the jungle they went
The more beautiful was his daughter.
The vast river on which they floated
Mirrored only one strand of her hair.
The tigers in the trees were nothing
But her short gasps of pleasure.

If the current slowed down more every day
It was because she was tired.
His conquest was wearing her out.
There was no room in her heart
For all of South America.

She died quietly, and the raft
Swung round like the second hand
Of a clock without hours,
Repeating in the middle of the river
The shape and process of a moment
From which there can be no escape.

The Poetry of Empire

for S. E. Carlisle

Your poems are ashamed
Of poetry, but you write them
Anyhow, in a special way
So they explode at the end
Like Cato's life.

I am also ashamed
As who would not be?—
Only an emperor
Can play the violin
In a burning empire.

We write less often
Than we used to. I
On days when the empire
Pauses and the world
Shows through, you

With the intermittence
Of a terrorist, who works
All week on the construction site
In order to buy
Her plastique.

After Dinner at the White House: A Photograph

Mr. Nixon is playing his spinet.
To his left, three consecutively smaller
Decorative Burmese fish
Smile into the corner from the wall.
An even smaller fish
Dangles from the lips of each.
Mr. Nixon gazes quizzically
In front of him at a white doe
Picking her delicate way beneath
The drooping lotus branches by the river bed.
Mid-Mozart, he's surprised
At the refinement of this oriental beast.
The President is looking delicate himself,
In fact his left hand droops
From his high wrist like a fish
That died before it left the hook,
Or like a lotus that perversely reaches
Not for the sun but for dark water
Where the doe's reflection stands
For light.

The President is thinking female
Just for now. Sherry, dinner
With an old friend, no TV—
The mood that comes upon him
In the grasscloth-papered sitting room
Is flowery and full of peace. In this cadenza
He imagines that he's Pat, his wife,
Covered in silk behind that pillar in Peking,
Graceful and shy, about to end
The war in Vietnam.

Just a Stage I'm Going Through

Neither death nor exile comes to you
Nor happens. They are performances
And long ones. The audience—
Eager, helpless, grieving—
Must be turned away one by one
Before you can lower your curtain
And disappear.

The alternative, of course,
Is immortality. The gaze
Of the audience transfixed
By the motionless body
Of an actor who cannot speak
His final line, who will not
Let them go home.

Fear of Travel

I'd be afraid to go to the desert,
That great ridged fingerprint
Of an indifferent God,
The land that actively abandons you
At every point.

Who would take care of me?
What if a sandstorm changed everything
During the night?

What could I make of such different life,
How could I ever remember it,
How could I tell you, afterwards?

The air was like the back room
Of a pizza shop in July
Crossed with the air of a laboratory.
The camel was like a horse
Which had just swallowed two swans.
The sounds were like paper
In a mechanical wind.
The sky was like the surface of a crucible
Full to the brim with a liquid that could kill.
There was no one there.
There was no one to talk to.
I wrote no letters because I forgot the alphabet,
Your names, the names of things
In the moist world through which I could lie to you
About what was here, what was left
After everything had been taken away.

Lines Written above the Mass Pike in Boston,
a Mile from the Ocean

On a bridge over the Mass Pike
In the full moon, among ragpickers,
The cars that come at you from the horizon
Grave as messengers, but faster,
Lighted like monuments, but faster,
Daring, but dignified, appear
To be at last the vision I've been waiting for
For years, the vision of adulthood:

The romance of them as they take the curves,
Their might and grace, the risks they take
Every second—so much weight, at such speed—
The distance they have come, the darkness
In which the driver sits at ease,
Accomplished, listening to the radio,
The nonchalance with which he stops
At the edge of the sea and turns off the machine,

The stillness then of the shore road,
The extra brightness of the moon
After the lights are off, the radio
Still playing as the driver, remembering
His body, gets out to stretch
And down at the water, the utmost East,
Turns back and sees the city, almost hears
The symphonic hum of the other arrivants,
Approaching the last exit.

Noise

I think I'm coming to the point
Where anything, anything at all
Would sound strange to me
And not just that dress rustling in the rubber plants
Or the click of gun and glass in the nearby saloon
The slight wheezing of the volcano on the horizon
The bells in the mission tower.

Now even the sound of the Audi Fox
Shifting gears near the park, where the branches creak
In a wind made simply by skyscrapers
Which creak also, and occasionally drop a window
With a liquid, gnashing sound—
Even that sound is strange
And the farther I travel home, the stranger.

The sound in my ears, now—
I can hear my brain beating. You can't.
For all you can hear this sound, I might as well
Be John Glenn, 100 miles up.
I wish I were. This world is all very well
But I want to hear mice on Mars
Scampering in a kind of dust
That won't bear thinking of.

This world is in rehearsal
Climbing its vast crescendo toward
That music you hear, three times in a lifetime,
At night, alone or not, and miles from anywhere,
As if the stars had turned to wire.

Flying to China

My friend, who cannot fly
And who drives her car oddly,
Flew me to China in a tiny airplane.
Six of us squeezed in
Where there was room
For three or four. Although
I am afraid of flying
I loved it, the dramatic banking,
The acute horizons. When I stood up
It was like surfing. Only heroes
Surf so high in the air.

I loved China too. It was winter
And an orange sunlight slanted in
Under the snowclouds, bright
But muffled, surreptitious.
While my friends sat inside
On the floor, in soft pajamas
Talking about love, I wandered
Among the little alleys
Where the whitest snow had drifted
Heavily against strange wooden houses,
Lacquered and windowless,
Low as the clouds, bright
As the secret light that filled
The air. There was no one there.
I was so happy to be alone in China
In this little low beauty, this distance.

I could hear the boats creaking in the river,
So close, in the intimate acoustics
Of the snowfall. But none of them
Could take me back as far
As I had come.

Why I Don't Publish in The New Yorker *(Yet)*

My window is obscured
By a sheet of plywood
Nailed to the frame.
I cannot even hear the birds
Gossip in the melancholy
Light of evening.
I cannot even read
The graffiti on the other side.

In the next house, I am too poor
To have a window. I live in the basement.
I have put a mirror
Where the window ought to be.
From time to time I dress up
As some trees or a bag lady
And perform "Spring Coming"
Or "Insouciant Poverty."

The office window reveals
An air shaft. (I call it "the courtyard,"
The superintendent refers to it as
"The atrium"; I have also heard "alley.")
There is no telling the season
Or the weather, or the time of day.
Basically, this window is a way
To use up excess glass.

Next time I move, I'll get a place
With a real window. I'll put a table
Next to it, and sit there writing poems
All day. Poems about the windows
Across the street, through which
I watch you fight and masturbate
And talk on the phone. Short, brutal
Poems about your life.

Uses of the Imperative

Stop grieving. Try on rage.
See how the wind of it
Explodes among the clouds
Announcing blue. Listen
To the fast new song of smithereens.
Let fire loose in the trash.
Hose down the mold of grief
Till your skin burns.
Grief colonized you like a virus.
Go swimming in blood.
Destroy what you can.

Does winter fester with the lost
Love of summer? No.
It kills everything in sight.
On the other side of the world
Enormous flowers rage
Into an opposing bloom.

U.S. Out of El Salvador, or, Amy & Bill 4-Ever

Has it ever occurred to you
That the people who write
On walls are organized?
That they are trying
To tell us something?
That if they didn't know something
Worth telling they wouldn't go out
In the cold and the dark and risk
Arrest to tell it? It's not like writing
Notes to yourself, you know.
It's bigger than TV, louder
Than poetry, harder to do
Than you might think, unless
You too have hung by your heels
Off the top of a water tower
Writing upside down in the dark
With a six-inch brush the name
Of the person you love
Or important instructions
To the government.

This literature is brief because
It takes so long to write.
It is written by hand because
It is written by persons.
It is unpublished because
It is so visible. It is full of love
For the reader, if love
Is what makes us speak
In spite of everything.
And its authors are organized:
It feels good to know
They are out there, hoarding and sharing

True history among themselves,
Burning with passion for each other
And for us, to whom they inscribe
So many messages, writ so large.

Elephant

When I dream of the Elephant
It is a dream of weight
And gravity. The world
Is in that dream, resting
On his back or trembling
Beneath his mighty feet.

In a painting of the Elephant
The world is his ornament—
Lively with continents,
The jewel of his office.
In play or dalliance
He tosses it to his mate.

Such moments, though, are rare.
Like Socrates, the strong-willed Elephant
Sleeps standing up
And lightly, dreaming of business.
Mountains and kingdoms totter
When he shifts his weight.

And yet, because he sleeps
He can be taken.
Sometimes the Elephant will lean
Against a tree for silent company.
If you cut down the tree, leap wide:
His fall is terrible, and you are small.

WARNING: NUCLEAR WASTE DUMP

This poem has to last
Ten thousand years
And be translated
Into every language
In the world.

Whoever conquers New Jersey
Must come equipped
With this poem, or die.

The poem must not depend
On music for its beauty
Since it must be equally beautiful
In every language
There will ever be.

It has to be so beautiful
That people will say it
For five hundred generations.
It must be universal
And timeless.

Millions of lives depend
On the beauty of this poem
But it cannot change
From ear to ear:

The critic who discovers
Its figurative sense
Must be silenced,
For the poem means
Exactly what it says.

We must find a way
To teach the birds
And the animals
To say it too,
And the trees, and water.

Precipitation

The snow was full of periwinkles.
It snowed even mussels last night
And oysters, and pearls:
Sea treasures. The firmament
Is upside down.

It snowed on the tropical rain forests
And this morning the shining eyes
Of the snakes peer out from under
Little hoods, like so many headlights
At rush hour, in stalled traffic
Here in the temperate zone.

It snowed on the pyramids, softening
Their imperial geometry
For the first time: all that fatal labor
Looks accidental now, just
Drifts, driven against the edge of the world.

The trash and foliage of the earth is hidden today.
The snow came from all over: it's total
And radical. Only the crusty keels of sunken galleons
Cut through the clouds that hover
Still: barnacles the size of stars
Fall in heaps on barns and monuments.

I Am Away from My House for the Week

The red tulips have fallen deeper toward satin,
The bird in his cage is bored and quiet.
Each day perhaps five sounds:
Two or three sudden sootfalls
On the kitchen windowsill,
A swell of suds rising in the sink
From the sink of my upstairs neighbor,
Tap of the creeper on the pane.
I left the light on in the hall—
Dim glow by day, dim glow by night,
Never enough to read by
Or to cook by, but too much for sleep.
The man whose windows
From across the lot face mine
Imagines in his fine heart
That I must be sad, or poor
Or very close to death.

"Light, may this be the last time I ever look at you!"

If the stars were eyes in the night sky
If the dark knots on the bark of the silver birch
In the dark wood were eyes
If the flat ovals of every still water
With their lashes of rush and grass
Were eyes looking into the sun's eye by day
The moon's roving eye by night
If the eyes of the wolf and the owl
Were eyes and not flames or broken mirrors
If the eyes of men and women
Were eyes and not wells, not windows
They would close, they would close.

The tired eyes of people and stars closing
The true dark at last, without gazes
Without watchfires, every lighthouse
Blinkered and the ships harbored
And sleep coming in with its final dream:
A song without words, and no one singing it.